Victoria Defined

You will not find Victoria
the place, marked on any map of London.

Victoria, the railway station, is part of
the busiest transport hub in the country.
Yet there is much more to Victoria, with its rich history,
fine architecture, parks and galleries, Victoria creates
an atmosphere that is distinctly different.

Victoria, the place, has no definitive boundaries.
It exists in our imagination and comprises
the areas of Belgravia, Pimlico and Westminster,
stretching across as far as Sloane Square to the west,
along Knightsbridge, to Parliament Square in the east
and down to the Thames.

Grosvenor, in partnership with Land Securities,
has produced 'Victoria Defined' as a
celebration of the area we know as Victoria.
The book reveals what for many will be a surprising
array of cultural riches, emphasising the vibrancy
that exists within Victoria, making it an attractive place
to live, work and have fun.

GROSVENOR

Victoria Defined

Two hundred years ago, the area of London we now call Victoria was a disparate collection of settlements. The heart of Westminster – the Abbey, Whitehall and the Palace of Westminster – was an important centre, but to the west of the Abbey were scattered fields, smallholdings, marshes, minor canalside industries and the odd cluster of cottages and pubs.

The area underwent a dramatic transformation in the nineteenth century. Vauxhall Bridge and new roads opened up large tracts of land. The brilliant developer Thomas Cubitt created the squares and terraces of Pimlico and Belgravia. Most crucially, two rail companies, the London,

Brighton & South Coast Railway, and the London, Chatham & Dover Railway, made Victoria the London terminus of their lines.

Victoria Station became the economic engine and the linchpin of the district. The building blocks were in place for the steady growth and evolution of one of London's most varied, vibrant areas.

Today Victoria is on the cusp of another important stage in its development. That is what makes 'Victoria Defined' such a timely contribution to understanding this diverse part of London.

From Fields
to Streets

A rich alchemy of architecture, businesses and
uses creates the best urban neighbourhoods,
explains Lance Knobel. Photographs by Phil Sayer

There is no easy formula for creating great cities. Some great cities thrive on density, others on green spaces. Some have dramatic skylines of tall buildings, others sprawl. What is certainly true, though, is that cities need a complex mix of elements to work. Areas that are undifferentiated – all homes or all offices – lack the constant vitality that fuels urban life. The best neighbourhoods have an alchemy of uses: interesting shops, a range of businesses, restaurants, cultural institutions, green spaces and a variety of housing.

Few parts of central London meet this high standard. Some areas are purely residential, others are dominated by retail use, while still others are office zones. This segregation was largely unplanned, the result of centuries of habit and development. But Victoria is different. Stretching from the Victorian Gothic of the Houses of Parliament to the elegant squares of Belgravia, the district combines some of the most historic sites in London, the busiest transport interchanges, some of the capital's most desirable housing, the Queen's primary residence, quiet parks and one of the world's great art galleries.

Perhaps because of this rich mix, Victoria does not have the clear identity of some of the other areas of central London. The City, for example, has long been one of the world's two most important financial districts, while Soho retains its reputation as a media village. Diversity is harder to pin down.

But for all the variation, there is a discernible structure to Victoria. The River Thames provides one boundary, St James's Park and Buckingham Palace a second, and the squares of Belgravia a third. The spine at the heart of Victoria is Victoria Street, created in 1847. When Victoria Station was built in 1860, Victoria Street became one of London's most important thoroughfares, linking a major rail terminus with the seat of political power in Whitehall.

Off this spine, Victoria is a mix of quiet streets with weighty residential blocks, smaller business developments and some attractive open spaces. Vincent Square, for example, hidden behind Vauxhall Bridge Road, is one of London's largest squares. The expansive playing fields in the middle are still for the use of the pupils of Westminster School, as they have been for many

Gothic and modern
The modernity of the Channel Four headquarters (right) contrasts with the Victorian Gothic of the Palace of Westminster (left)

Victoria is different. It combines historic sites, transport interchanges, desirable housing and quiet parks

The fields were used for artillery
practice, remembered through the
name of Artillery Row

centuries. Even earlier, the fields in this area were used for artillery practice, remembered through the name of nearby Artillery Row.

Tucked away in these streets are a wealth of intriguing places to shop and eat. Elizabeth Street, which runs from Victoria Station into the heart of Belgravia, is a rich cluster of specialist shops and small restaurants. Couture hat maker Philip Treacy shares the pavement with the shop of the Chocolate Society. And the best bread in the world comes from the only Poilâne bakery outside Paris.

Around the corner off Grosvenor Gardens, The Goring hotel is a survivor of a different era – a small luxury hotel run by the same family for four generations. Its proximity to Buckingham Palace has led to some distinguished guests: the Crown Prince of Norway once told the hoteliers, "I much prefer to stay at The Goring. I don't have a bathroom to myself in Buckingham Palace."

The largest presence in the district, however, is undoubtedly Victoria Station. From the ground, it would be easy to overlook the importance of the station to the area.

Step into the past
Unusual corners are hidden in back streets. Cockpit Steps (left) was the site of cock fights in the 17th and 18th centuries, when the towers of Westminster Abbey (above) were being completed by Nicholas Hawksmoor

It is hemmed in by buildings, and the broad swathe of tracks is disguised by the terraced housing of Pimlico. But the station, the busiest in London with 85 million passengers a year, anchors the dense transport infrastructure of the district. In addition to the main railway lines, Victoria is an interchange for three of the major London Underground routes: the Circle, District and Victoria lines. Other stations on these lines provide the Victoria area with a dense web of connections.

It's hard to imagine the transformative power of a major train station on an urban area. When Victoria Station was built in 1860, the railway lines caused surprisingly little disruption, since they were built over the Grosvenor Canal. But upon completion, the "course of civilisation and improvement" meant that people could stream straight into the centre of London, providing workers for the offices and customers for the shops. Some developers responded immediately to the new impetus. The Grosvenor Hotel, built alongside Victoria Station in 1860-62, was the greatest hotel London had yet seen. The new terminus also spurred development along

Victoria Street. Most enduring, perhaps, was the Army & Navy Stores, set up in 1871 by a cooperative of officers to provide military men and their families with discount provisions. Not long after, in 1884, Cardinal Manning, the second Archbishop of Westminster, bought land just off Victoria Street to erect Westminster Cathedral.

So it's not surprising that Victoria has long been an important centre for business in London. Today the area harbours a diverse group of companies, ranging from aerospace group Rolls-Royce, the world's second largest manufacturer of jet engines, to BHP Billiton, the world's biggest mining group, to John Lewis Partnership, one of Britain's major retailers, to book publishers Random House, to internet leader Yahoo Europe.

Some parts of Victoria are among the most historic in London. Westminster Abbey probably dates to King Offa in the eighth century, while next door Edward the Confessor started the Palace of Westminster in 1050. Their proximity is not coincident: Edward started the palace as part of a precinct including church, monastery and palace. It's a sign of the balance of power in the

Throes of change
Victoria Station (left and previous pages) is London's busiest transport hub. New developments (right) are provoking further transformation of the area

The largest presence in the district, however, is undoubtedly Victoria Station

The most fashionable streets of
Georgian London were in St James's,
but Victoria had its share

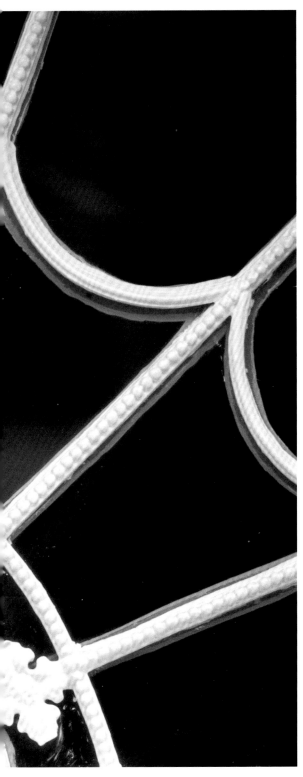

11th century that the church clearly had the better site, away from the flood-prone Thames.

These medieval foundations have supported many generations of building. In the 13th century under Henry III, the Abbey's most memorable architecture was completed (although the distinctive towers are an 18th-century addition). The Palace has an even more fitful history.

It survived Guy Fawkes's Gunpowder Plot in 1605, but fire destroyed much of it in 1834. This provided the impetus for a competition for new Houses of Parliament on the site. Charles Barry

and the grandly named Augustus Welby Northmore Pugin are responsible for the stately Gothic building that now provides the image of parliamentary democracy.

Given these two monumental works, it is a puzzle that this area of London did not fully develop until well into the 19th century, when most of the rest of the city boomed in the 18th century. Some historians point to the Dean and Chapter of the Abbey, which owned much of the land. They were conservative landlords, content with its fields and smallholders. And in Georgian

Georgian grandeur
Queen Anne's Gate (left and above) remains one of London's great Georgian streets. The buildings retain their Coade Stone porches. A statue of Queen Anne surveys the scene. Around the corner (following pages) the Changing of the Guard at Buckingham Palace

London's building boom, fashion spurred areas to the north, clustering around the court at St James's. Part of the reason was also practical: much of what is now Victoria was low-lying and subject to flooding.

One of the district's most distinctive buildings, St John's, Smith Square (now a concert hall), had a building history plagued by the marshy land. The architect, Thomas Archer, struggled with the soggy foundations, which was part of the reason why it was the costliest of the churches built under the 1711 Fifty Churches Act.

However slow the district was to develop, in the 19th century it was completely transformed. The building of Vauxhall Bridge in 1816 and the creation of Vauxhall Bridge Road opened up the southern stretches of the area. But the real leap forward came with Thomas Cubitt's development of Pimlico and Belgravia.

Other developers had tried to plan the area, but had always been defeated by the many plots of land owned by different estates. Cubitt was able to tie together deals with the Grosvenor Estate, the Crown Estate and other land owners to realise a master plan. From the 1820s to the

1850s, he turned the fields, factories and swamps into a desirable place to live for London's rising middle class.

Fifty years after he first signed the agreements to redevelop the area, one London newspaper would describe what was then known as South Belgravia: "Here are squares and churches. South Belgravia is genteel, sacred to professional men of various grades, not rich enough to luxuriate in Belgravia proper, but rich enough to live in private houses – for this is a retired suburb. Here people are more lively than in Kensington, though not so grand, of course, as in Albertopolis, and yet a cut above Chelsea, which is only commercial, and ever so much more respectable than Westminster, dreadfully behind the age, vegetating the other side of the Vauxhall-bridge road." Cubitt was also responsible for developing the far grander Grosvenor Estate lands in Belgravia, including Eaton Square and Belgrave Square, probably London's most sought-after addresses. His influence on Victoria doesn't end here, however. In 1846 Cubitt was commissioned to carry out the enlargement of Buckingham Palace, to the designs of Edward Blore. Much of

Fashion and filigree
Elegant shops like Ben de Lisi (left) and antique dealers (right) cluster around Ebury Street and Pimlico Road, just south-west of Victoria Station

The real leap forward came with Thomas Cubitt's development of Pimlico and Belgravia

Some of London's grandest mansion blocks cluster in the streets around Westminster Cathedral

the palace seen today is Cubitt's work, although the east front – the public face of the palace – was tacked on in 1913 by Sir Aston Webb.

The comprehensive redevelopment by Cubitt of such a large area is a project that can never be repeated in a city like London. Today change comes about through more strategic interventions rather than wholesale clearing of districts.

That is what is happening in Victoria now. Cardinal Place, at the Victoria Station end of Victoria Street, is the first of a planned series of developments that promise to extend the rich mix of the district. Cardinal Place will create public open spaces, together with new retail and offices. Nearby, further development is planned to include residential elements to maintain the diversity of the area. On the other side of Victoria Station, too, major office developments are providing a clearer texture to the district.

Over the coming decade, much of Victoria looks likely to be transformed into something well tuned to the needs of contemporary London.

Brick and stone
Behind Westminster Cathedral, the streets are crowded with some of London's grandest mansion blocks (left). Boys at Westminster School (above) learn to take the history surrounding them in their stride

Victoria's vintage:
The Goring hotel,
renowned for its wine
list and traditional
restaurant, acclaimed by
Egon Ronay and Michelin,
is a peaceful oasis in
which to escape the busy
centre of London

The Good Life

Hidden behind simple doors or down the side streets are Victoria's delights: cooking, entertainment and service to rival anything in the capital. Photographs by Simon Wheeler

Royal families often use The Goring hotel as a home from home when they are visiting nearby Buckingham Palace. And royalty are not the only VIPs to take the oldest privately owned hotel in London to their heart. "To stay anywhere else in London is inconceivable to me. It would be like snubbing a favourite nanny," actor Christopher Plummer said.

Built in an elegant Edwardian Baroque style, it was the first hotel in the world to offer central heating and a bathroom for every bedroom. Its critically acclaimed dining room, garden bar and relaxed traditionality have maintained its place in the affection of a variety of visitors.

Otto Richard Goring founded the hotel in 1910 and ownership remains in the same family today, with the founder's grandson George Goring at the helm. It would be difficult for George's connection to the hotel to be any closer. He was born there in 1938, and started work there in 1962. He was elected British Hotelier of the Year in 1990 and received an OBE from the Queen in 1992 for service to the hotel industry.

Dignified friend: The Goring's genteel but relaxed atmosphere has helped maintain its place in the affections of a variety of visitors, including royalty and actors, since 1910

The Goring

St John's,
Smith Square

St John's, Smith Square, stands proudly on the eastern reaches of Victoria, separated from the River Thames by Millbank. It is home to the Academy of Ancient Music and one of London's best concert venues.

Built in 1728 to a design by Thomas Archer, legend has it that Queen Anne kicked over her footstool and told the architect to build it "like that!". With its four towers looking indeed like stool legs, it has been called Queen Anne's Footstool ever since. Charles Dickens described it as "some petrified monster". But it came to be recognised as one of the finest examples of English Baroque architecture. The renowned art historian Nikolaus Pevsner described it as "the boldest manifestation of English Baroque in Inner London, spectacularly independent".

After being severely damaged in the Second World War it was deconsecrated and restored as a concert hall, and regained its grandeur with aplomb. In 1981 Sir Hugh Casson wrote, "To... listen to fine music within its walls is an experience not to be matched in conventional concert halls."

Face the music:
the Isis Trio rehearse
for one of the much-
loved lunchtime
performances at
a concert hall that
is internationally
respected thanks to its
majestic appearance
and impressive
acoustics

Having been awarded the Médaille d'Or in 1994 and a Michelin award in 1993 for a chain of Lebanese brasseries in France, the Bou Antoun brothers Nader and Jean-Paul opened London's Noura in 1999.

Nader and Jean-Paul started work in the restaurant business in the early 1970s in Lebanon. After quickly making a success of their chosen careers, they opened a 30-seat restaurant in Paris in 1980. Within a few years they moved to new premises with 110 seats.

Noura's menu includes aubergine dishes, hoummous, falafel, sfeeha (a Lebanese pizza with minced lamb), ferri (grilled quail) and chicken chawarma. There are also Lebanese wines, such as Château Musar. The *Independent* newspaper confirms Noura's qualities: "With sleek, chrome, curved lines and muted beige and grey interior, this is like an ocean liner. The outstanding cuisine of the Levant is the order of the day. Orange blossom, rosewater and mango ice creams make a memorable ending."

Creative kitchen: the authentic flavours and evocative aromas of Lebanese cooking complement the buzz of an exciting, modern brasserie. Delectable mezze (following pages) and hot flatbreads start the feast

Noura

Boisdale

Ranald Macdonald has always been a jazz enthusiast, so after he opened Boisdale of Belgravia in 1988 he established regular band performances there to complement the traditional, club-like feel of the restaurant and bar. A deep sense of his personal history fills every corner, from the Macdonald Bar, opened in June 1999 with its seven-metre zinc bar to serve an extensive array of cocktails, to the name of the restaurant: Boisdale is a loch on the Hebridean island of Uist, the original home of the Macdonald family.

"Customers at Boisdale don't come to listen to the music with a reverential attitude; they talk, laugh, often dance and smoke," Macdonald says. There is a renowned list of 17 brands and more than 110 different sizes and vintages of Cuban cigars.

A distinctive personality is stamped on each room. Visitors can enjoy the flowers in the Courtyard Garden before retiring to the Back Bar in a mews cottage. The restaurant is at the heart of it all, with head chef David Morey and an award-winning wine list.

Scotland meets Havana: table talk in a unique world of jazz, Caledonian and Latin food, generous lists of wines, whiskies or rums and mountains of lovingly chosen Cuban cigars

Poilâne

More than 3,000 people in the United States love a particular French bread so much that they insist on it being delivered to them regularly by Federal Express. Frank Sinatra had the same bread flown to his breakfast table every morning, wherever he happened to be. People in Victoria do not have to go to such lengths to get hold of a loaf. They simply visit Poilâne on Elizabeth Street.

Poilâne's London bakery, simple and gimmick-free, is an exact replica of its Paris counterpart on the fashionable rue du Cherche-Midi. Bread and other delicacies, such as rye, nut or raisin bread, brioches, croissants, pains au chocolat and apple tarts, are freshly baked every day on the premises. It is a practice that has worked well since Pierre Poilâne first opened in Paris in 1932.

Poilâne makes traditional French bread, using only wheat flour, ground by stone milling to produce sourdough, giving the bread its distinctive flavour. The founder's granddaughter Apollonia now runs the business and continues a grand tradition.

A place in history: for three generations, the French Poilâne family has baked amazing breads using its ancestral recipes, including sourdough

Handled with care:
the bakers gently shelve
each newly created
loaf to await delivery
or collection

TIN MOULDS FOR SWEETS, SAVOURIES.

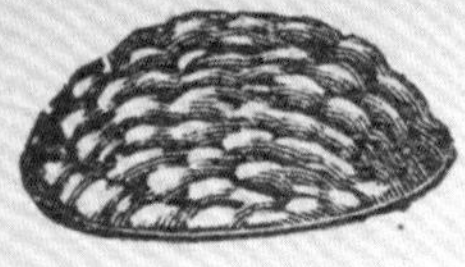
T.G.I. 453.
Walnut 5 in.
Doz. 1/6

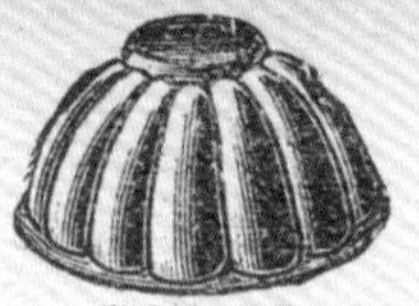
T.G.I. 455.
Cup, 2½ in.
Doz. 2/-

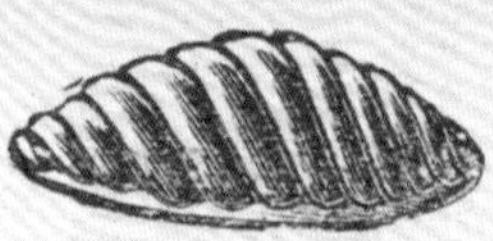
T.G.I. 457.
Quenelle Shell, 2⅝ in.
Doz. 1/3

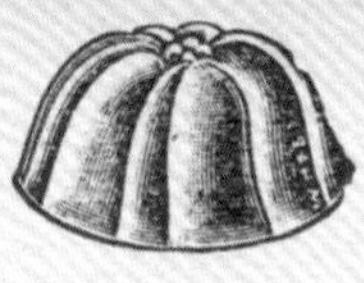
T.G.I. 459.
Apple .. doz. 2/3

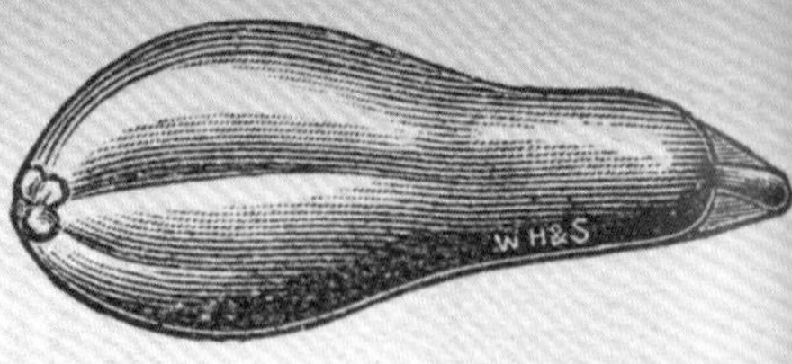
T.G.I. 461.
Pear, 3 in.
Doz. 1/9

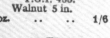

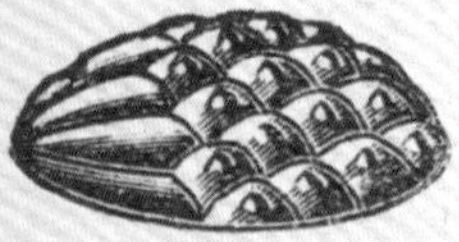
T.G.I. 454.
Oval, 3 in.
Doz. ... 2/3

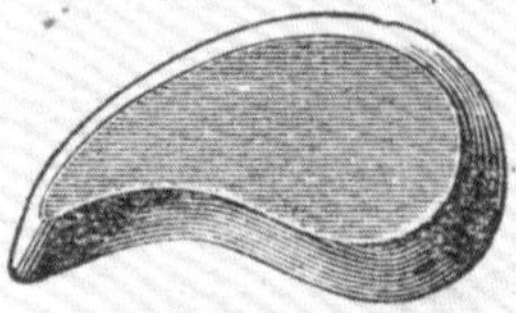
T.G.I. 456.
Cutlet Pans, 3⅜ in.
Doz. 1/3

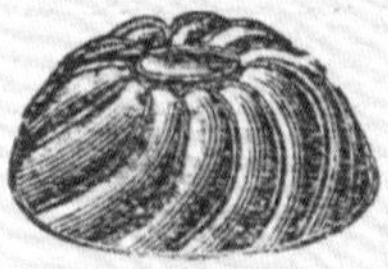
T.G.I. 458.
Bouché Cup.
Doz. 2/3

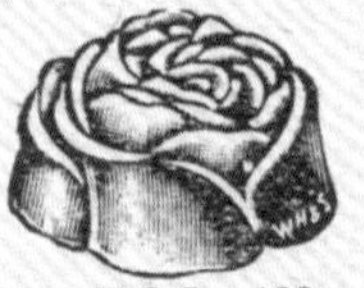
T.G.I. 460
Rose.
Doz. .. 2/3

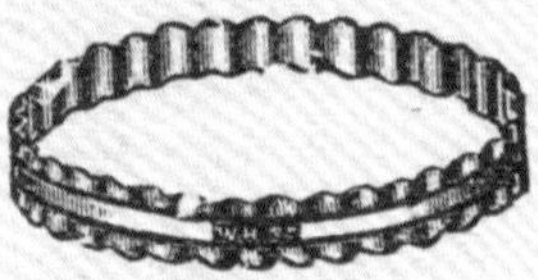
T.G.I. 462.
Fluted Fleur Rings, 7 in., 1/4 each; 6 in., 1/3. Plain, 7 in., -/9; 6 in., -/8

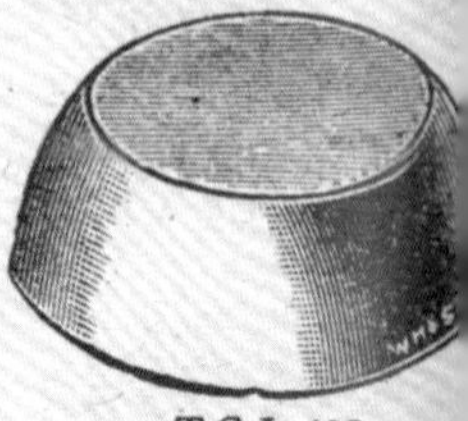
T.G.I. 463.
Bouché Cup, Plain.
1½, 1⅝, and 2 in.
Doz. 2

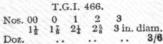

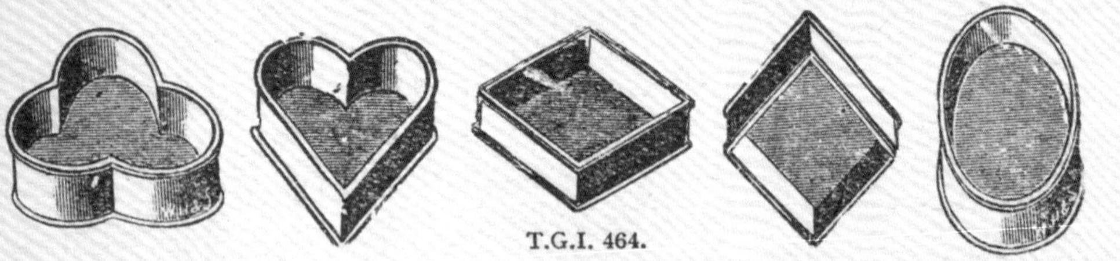
T.G.I. 464.
Queen's Cake Moulds, Hearts, Clubs, Crescents, Round, Diamonds, Ovals, Squares, doz. 2/6

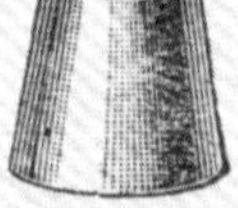
Plain Dariol Cups
T.G.I. 465.

Nos.	00	0	1	2	3
	1⅝	1¾	2	2¼	2½ in. diam.
Doz.	..	..	..	..	3/-

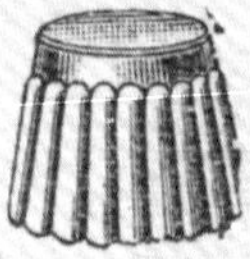
Fluted Dariol Cups.
T.G.I. 466.

Nos.	00	0	1	2	3
	1½	1⅞	2¼	2⅝	3 in. diam.
Doz.	..	..	..	..	3/6

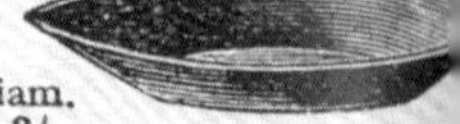
T.G.I. 467.
Boat Patties.
2¼, 3, and 4 in.
Doz. .. ..

TIN MOULDS.

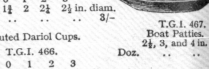

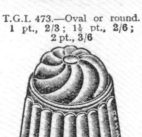

T.G.I. 468. **ALUMINIUM CINDERELLA BISCUIT MOUL** made in seven shapes for making Pastry. Cases can be filled Jams, Jellies, Meat, Fish, etc. .. .. each

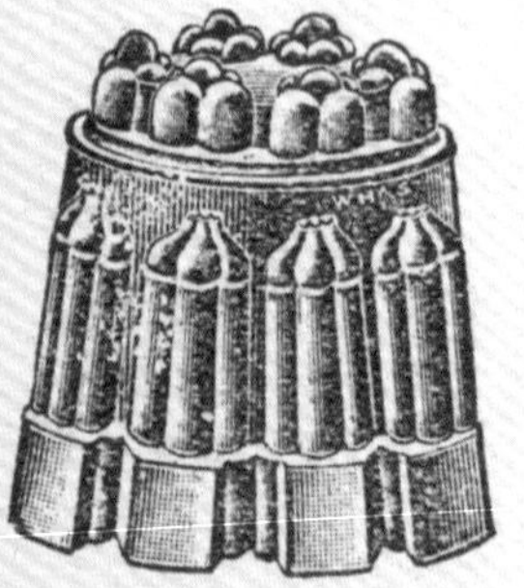
T.G.I. 469.—Oval.
1 pt., 2/3; 1½ pt., 2/6; 2 pt., 3/6

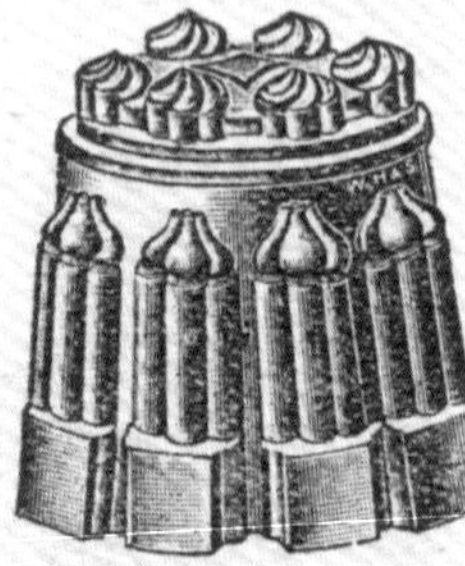
T.G.I. 473.—Oval or round.
1 pt., 2/3; 1½ pt., 2/6; 2 pt., 3/6

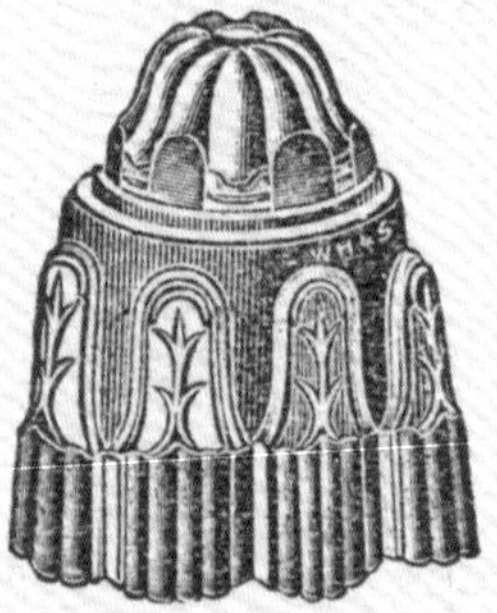
T.G.I. 477.—Round.
1 pt., 2/3; 1½ pt., 2/6; 2 pt., 3/6

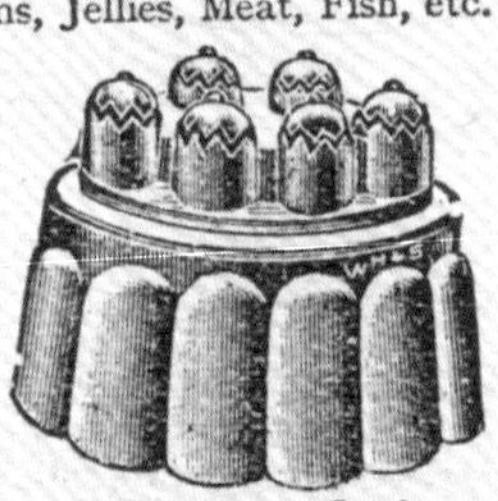
T.G.I. 481.—Oval.
1½ pt., 3/-; 2 pt., 3/6

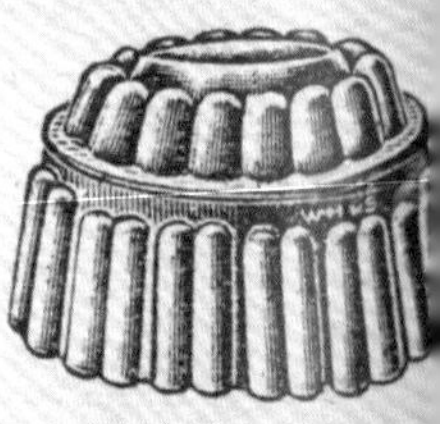
T.G.I. 485.—Oval.
1½ pt., 2/6; 2 pt., 3

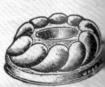

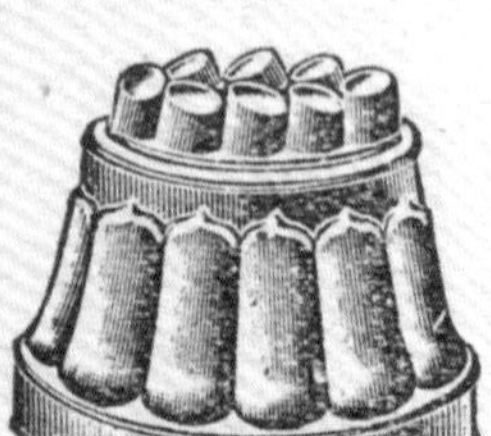
T.G.I. 470.—Oval.
2 pt., 3/-; 2½ pt., 3/6; 3 pt., 4/-

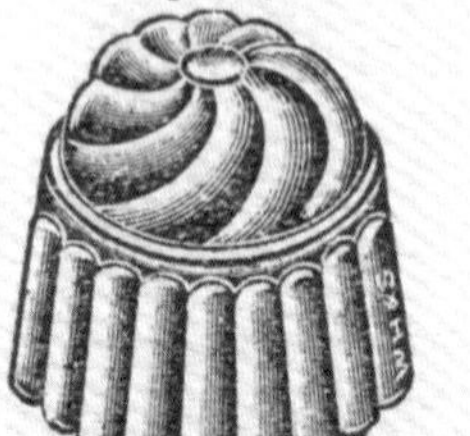
T.G.I. 474.—Round.
½ pt. .. .. each 1/-

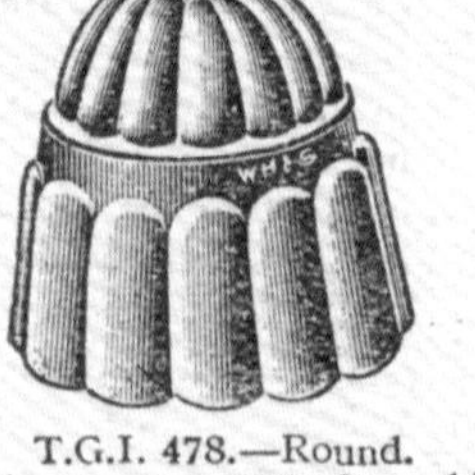
T.G.I. 478.—Round.
½ pt. .. .. each 1/-
¾ „ .. .. „ 1/3

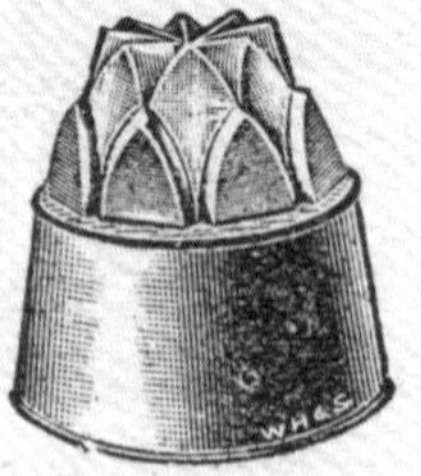
T.G.I. 482.—Round.
½ pt. .. .. each 1/-

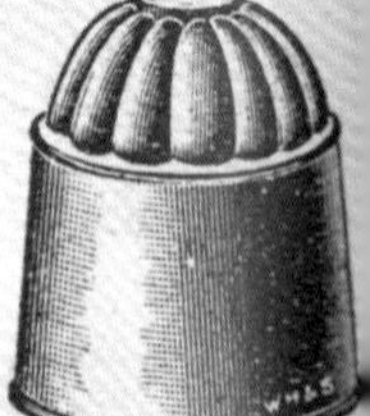
T.G.I. 486—Round.
½ pt., 1/-; ¾ pt., 1/3

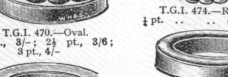

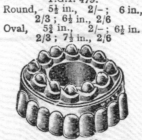

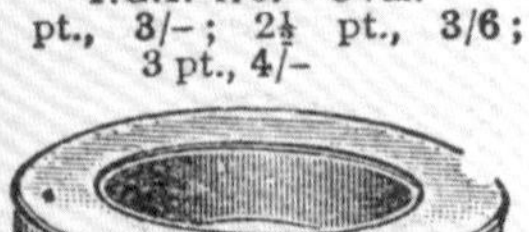
T.G.I. 471.
Border, oval, plain.
Length, 5¾ in., 2/-; 6¾ in., 2/3; 7¼ in., 2/6
Do., round, plain.
Diam., 5½ in., 2/-; 6 in., 2/3; 6½ in., 2/6

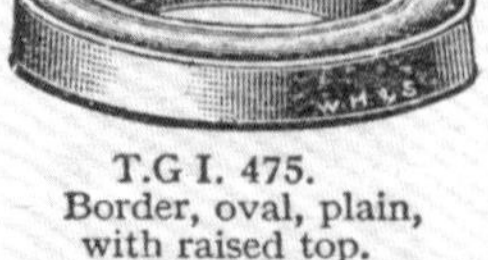
T.G.I. 475.
Border, oval, plain, with raised top.
Length, 5¾ in., 2/-; 6¾ in., 2/3; 7¼ in., 2/6
Do., round, plain, with do.
Diam., 5½ in., 2/-; 6 in., 2/3; 6½ in., 2/6

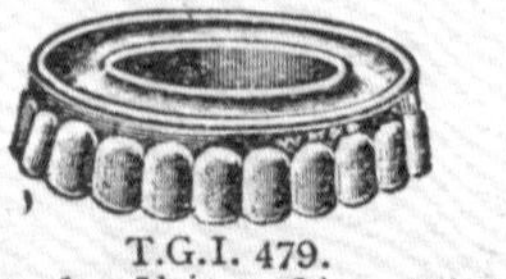
T.G.I. 479.
Round, 5½ in., 2/-; 6 in., 2/3; 6½ in., 2/6
Oval, 5¾ in., 2/-; 6½ in. 2/3; 7¼ in., 2/6

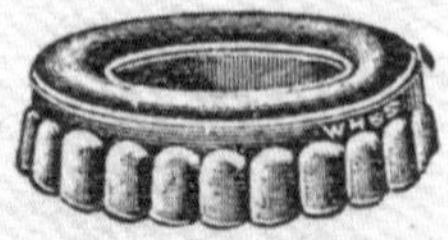
T.G.I. 483
Round, 5½ in., 2/-; 6 in., 2/3; 6½ in., 2/6
Oval, 5¾ in., 2/-; 6½ in., 2/3; 7½ in., 2/6

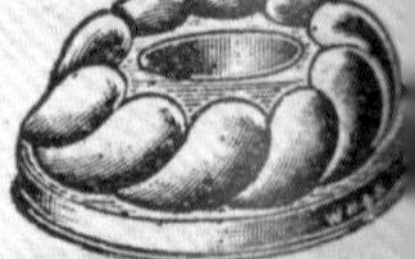
T.G.I. 487.—Trois F
4 in., 3/9; 5 in., 4/9
5½ in., 5/-

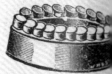

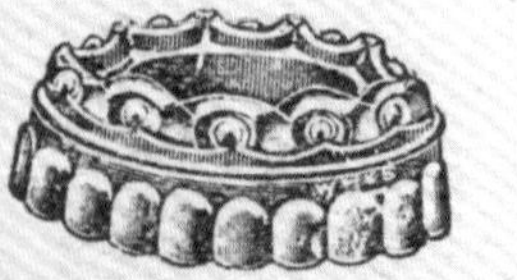
T.G.I. 472.
Oval Border Mould.
7¼ in., 3/9

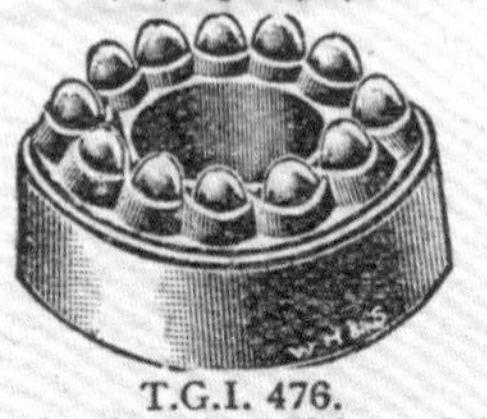
T.G.I. 476.
Oval, length, 5¾ in., 3/3; 6½ in., 3/9; 7 in., 4/3
Round, length, 5¼ in., 3/3; 6 in., 3/9; 6½ in., 4/3

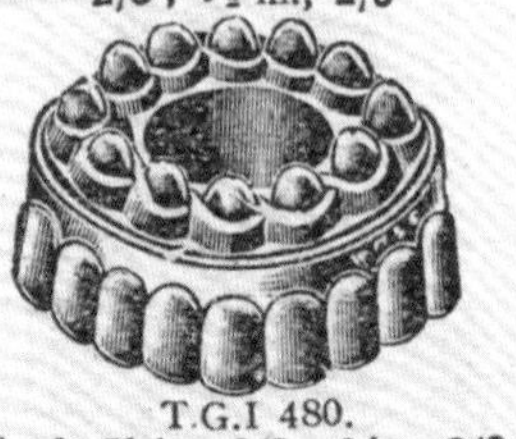
T.G.I. 480.
Oval, 5½ in., 3/3; 6 in., 3/9; 6½ in., 4/3
Round, 5 in., 3/3; 5½ in., 3/9; 6 in., 4/3

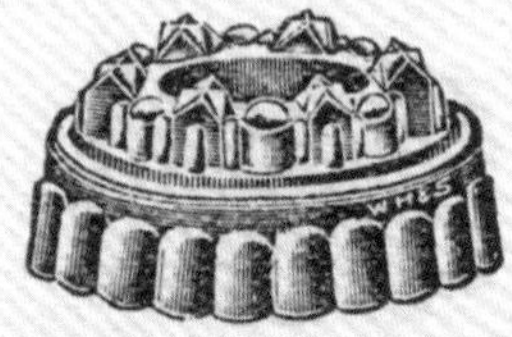
T.G.I. 484.
Oval Border Mould.
5¾ in., 3/-; 6½ in., 3/6; 7 in., 4/3

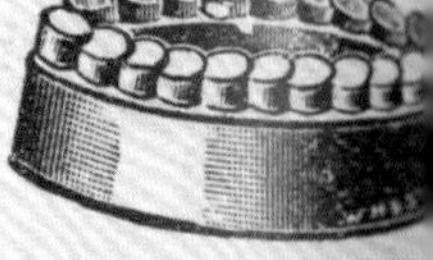
T.G.I. 488.—Oval bor
5½ in., 3/3; 6 in., 3/
7 in., 4/3

ALL PRICES ARE SUBJECT TO MARKET FLUCTUATIONS.

Army & Navy

The mail order catalogue of the Army & Navy Stores
was the virtual emporium for the British Empire.
Unable to visit the great store on Victoria Street,
families in Calcutta, Cape Town or Cairo could order
everything necessary to maintain their all-important
appearances, from furniture to jelly moulds

From big streets to small, Lucinda Rogers' drawn tour of Victoria

Street Life

Dean's Yard (previous page)
Walk through a Victorian Gothic archway to the side of Westminster Abbey's main entrance and you enter the tranquillity of Dean's Yard, a small cathedral close-like oasis in the centre of London. The buildings are a hodge-podge – some as old as the 14th century, others as recent as 1940. The east side of the Yard (illustrated) is mostly from the late 14th century and now belongs principally to Westminster School, one of the great schools of England. Former students have included Ben Jonson, Christopher Wren, Charles Dodgson (Lewis Carroll) and John Gielgud.

Victoria Street coffee shop (below)
With thousands of office workers in the buildings that range the length of Victoria Street, it is unsurprising that coffee shops, sandwich bars and pubs are popular.

Blewcoat School (right)
Tucked between large, modern office blocks, the charming brown-and-red-brick Blewcoat School is a remarkable survivor in an area that has undergone such enormous change. Founded nearby in 1688, it was rebuilt on its present site in Caxton Street in 1709 for the owner of the once-famous Stag Brewery. In 1954 the school was bought by the National Trust. The single big schoolroom inside is now used as its shop.

Central Hall Westminster (previous page)

In 1898 the Methodist Church set out to raise one million guineas from one million Methodists to commemorate the centenary of John Wesley's death. Much of the money went to the construction of the imposing Central Hall, completed in 1912. The suffragettes met here in 1914, Mahatma Gandhi spoke to the Temperance Movement in 1931, and Charles de Gaulle announced the founding of the Free French forces in 1940. Most famously, the first General Assembly of the United Nations was held in Central Hall in 1946, with 51 countries sending delegations.

Carlisle Mansions (below)

To the south of Westminster Cathedral, Victorian mansion blocks of flats crowd the streets. Carlisle Mansions, 1885-89, is one of the grandest and most decorative.

The Grenadier (right)

Tucked behind Belgravia's squares are the modest mews, which once served as stables. In Wilton Row is the Grenadier pub whose name harks back to an army guards' barracks that was nearby until 1835.

Farmers' Market (overleaf)

On Saturday mornings, Pimlico Road hosts one of London's largest farmers' markets, with producers from all over Britain selling fresh fruit and vegetables, meat, fish, baked goods and flowers.

Channel 4

Britain's state-owned commercial broadcaster has a remit to provide innovative, experimental and creative programming. From its spectacular Richard Rogers-designed offices on Horseferry Road, Channel 4 operates like a publisher, commissioning all its work from independent production companies

Victoria's shops hold some of
London's most desirable objects.
Interviews by Daniel Lee.
Photographs by Helen Mellor

Treasure Trove

Run and Become

Taking personal care of runners

I like to think I understand runners, being a runner myself and having done the New York marathon three times. Exercise is important to my family. My father has been a keen runner for a long time and ran a marathon last year, even though he is in his mid-sixties."

Thirty-one-year-old Shankara Smith explains what sets apart specialist running-shoe shop Run and Become. Tucked away in bustling, pedestrianised Palmer Street is the shop's metal and glass frontage. Running shoes stacked in neat rows round the windows, pictures of an Eastern guru and meditative music give the shop the feel of a temple.

Smith owns the shop and its Edinburgh and Cardiff sites with three other members of the Smith family: her father, Tony, who started the business in 1982; her mother Cherry; and her younger sister Dipika. Shankara says: "My father was inspired to open the shop by his meditation teacher Sri Chinmoy, whose teachings emphasise the importance of exercise for meditation and a healthy mind. This ethos runs through everything we do, whether we are dealing with families, first-time runners or sports professionals.

"Choosing the right shoe for the shape of your foot and different running surfaces is essential. The street comes to life at lunchtimes, when lots of customers rush in with different-shaped feet and all sorts of requirements, from marathons to fell running. Our stock ranges from £35 track shoes to the £110 Asics Kayano road-running shoe. Being in the centre of a city the most common request is for shoes to run on concrete surfaces.

"Most of our customers are fairly sophisticated and because we are near to the Houses of Parliament we get a fair number of politician customers, such as (foreign secretary) Jack Straw and (former Blair communications chief) Alastair Campbell. There are other well-known faces, such as celebrity chef Gordon Ramsay and comedian Lenny Henry.

"We make sure that all of the 14 members of staff at the shop, as well as our people in Edinburgh and Cardiff, have a feel for running. Adrian Stott, for example, the manager of our Edinburgh store, is on the British team for ultra-distance races. With people like him on our team we hope there's no chance of us letting anyone choose the wrong shoe.

J Wippell and Company

Craftsmanship for churchmen

We first opened a London shop in 1898 in Charing Cross before moving to the current building in Victoria in 1930. It has always had a close link with the church and it was built by the Church Commissioners in 1904 as the Westminster Female Refuge, to deal with fallen women," explains Gerald Miller, chairman and managing director of J Wippell and Company.

Wippells, ecclesiastical outfitters and church furnishers, is a family institution. It has remained in Wippell hands since the early 19th century and displays its deep sense of tradition with carefully crafted religious artefacts, such as a golden-eagle lectern, at its Tufton Street shop in the shadow of Westminster Abbey.

Originating in Exeter, Devon, where it still has its head office, it also has stores in Manchester and abroad in New Jersey. All 30 shareholders in the company are Wippell family members, but 70-year-old Gerald Miller is not. He joined the company 50 years ago. Miller says: "Craftsmanship is at the heart of everything we do and Wippells wanted to make this clear when it moved to Tufton Street. It built the shop-front from English oak, with bas-relief carvings on each side

of the door. One is a stone mason to represent our business and the other is a female spinster, relating to the original use of the building.

"Our clientele is not only ecclesiastical. Anyone can buy from us. We make academic gowns and we also made Princess Alexandra's Lancaster University chancellor's gown. Clearly, though, religious work is a major part of our business and we have made gowns for most of the notables in the Anglican communion, including Archbishop Tutu.

"As well as robes and church furniture, we also make stained glass and are currently working on a large west window for St Paul's Cathedral in Victoria, Seychelles. As time has moved on we have updated our techniques, using computers today and taking on business around the globe, but we have continued to emphasise our craftsmanship.

"At a recent Lambeth conference (where Anglican leaders from around the world meet) debating lots of changes for the church, the bishop of Western Australia reportedly said the only thing unchanging in the Anglican community was Wippell and Company.

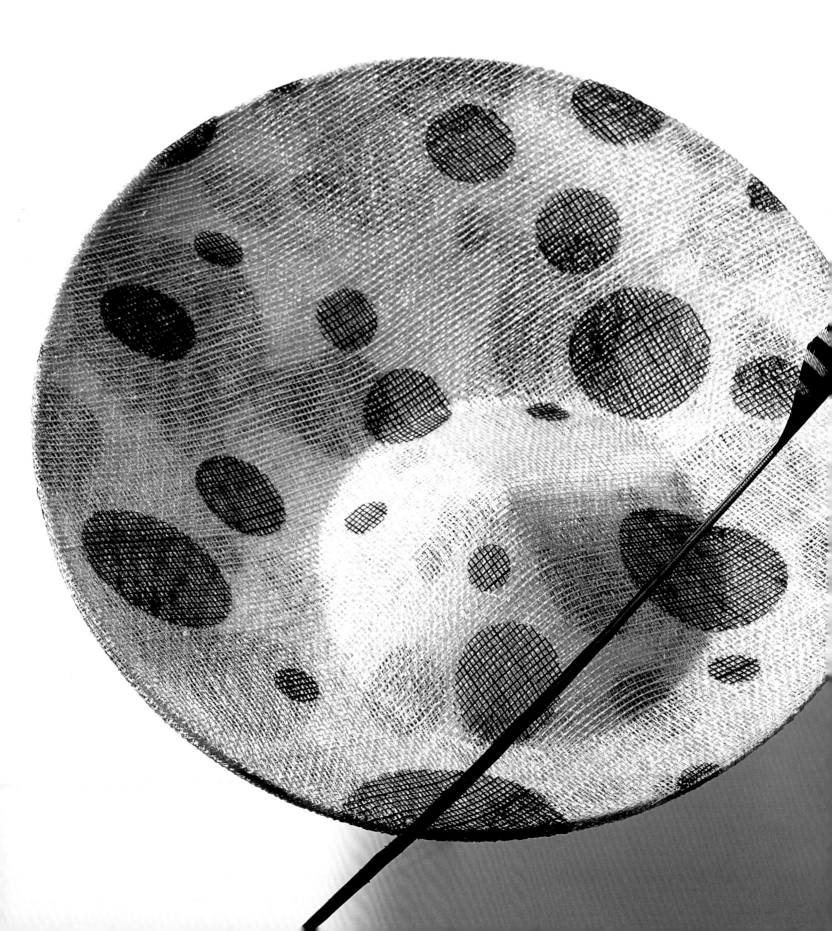

"I love my work and my shop, but Mr Pig, my Jack Russell dog, is the real presence on this street. He sits in the window and watches each customer. He's a real character, and everyone knows him. Even though it's the centre of London, this area has the friendly feel of my home village in Ireland," says haute couture accessory designer Philip Treacy, winner of numerous awards.

Village life and hats have always been important to Treacy. Born in a tiny village in the west of Ireland in 1967, his home gave him a bird's-eye view of the village church and its endless displays of wedding hats.

After studying fashion, he started a 10-year stint designing hats for Karl Lagerfeld at Chanel when he was just 23 and his work is now always a presence at big hat events, such as Royal Ascot. In 1994 he opened his own wonderland of a shop on Elizabeth Street, filled with elegant mannequins and every kind of shape of hat imaginable. Philip says: "It is good to feel as

though I'm still in a village, because that's where I began to like working with my hands as a child. I loved making things. I love making something from nothing, turning two-dimensional material into something three-dimensional. That's why I design bags as well as hats, and I've also been asked to design a hotel interior.

"Most of my work is designed for specific events, for specific people, from Marilyn Manson to Diana Ross and members of the Royal Family. I feel very privileged because not only have I been able to change people's perceptions of the hat, putting it back at the heart of fashion, but a hat can also make people smile. The face is such a potent part of a person, the part you talk to and watch, and a hat can make it look completely different.

"But, in the end I don't do this for the glamour. I do it because I really enjoy it. That's why I was into creating things as a child, because I could do something impressive, even though I didn't know why – a sort of party trick.

Philip Treacy
Making hats fashionable again

David Mellor

Designs that work well and look good

Cutlery has always been our main product, dating back to when my father designed his first range – Pride – while he was still a student at the Royal College of Art in 1953. It was manufactured by Walker & Hall," explains Corin Mellor.

The David Mellor kitchenware and tableware shop, full of careful displays of everything a cook could want, has been a modern, glass landmark on the corner of Sloane Square since it opened in 1969. Its sleek cutlery is admired throughout the world.

Born in 1930 in Sheffield, then the centre of British steel production, David Mellor is a Royal Designer for Industry and has been called the cutlery king. The company has shops around the country as well as its own factory. David runs the business with his daughter Clare, his wife Fiona and his son Corin. Thirty-seven-year-old Corin, trained as a furniture designer, says: "A lot of people do not know that my father has always been involved in all sorts of designs that have nothing to do with the kitchen. In the mid-60s, for example, he designed new traffic signals with the Ministry of Transport.

"His designs have had a huge effect. When he started designing, stainless steel was a relatively new material and it is partly thanks to him that it became so fashionable.

"Today, we get a lot of famous names in the shop, from TV cook Nigella Lawson to footballer David Beckham, but sometimes you have to be careful to recognise who you are dealing with. My father once insisted that a customer sign for a purchase when she didn't want to. She was Jackie Onassis.

"We have always been keen to ensure that our products work well and look good. From our award-winning factory, purpose-designed by Sir Michael Hopkins in the Peak National Park, to our shop displays, we try to balance form and function.

"We have a visitor centre at the factory so that people can see how everything is made, because that is part of understanding its beauty. I used to be fascinated by watching my father making things when I was as young as five years old. That's why I wanted to come into this business and hopefully other people will feel as inspired.

Appley Hoare

Furniture and flowers for Francophiles

I like to think of my furniture and other pieces as having rustic charm. We may clean them up, but we leave them in enough of their original state for people to be able to see their history and the hands that have touched them over decades," says Appley Hoare.

Picture a French country garden filled with rustic furniture, sculptures and coloured flowers and you will not be too far from the look of Appley Hoare antiques and flowers. In two shops knocked into one, the eponymous Appley Hoare deals with the antiques, while her daughter Zoë takes care of the flowers.

Appley spent 20 years in Australia, where she wrote a magazine column on interiors and specialised in French pieces, before moving back to the country of her birth in 1999 to open her shop on London's fashionable Pimlico Road. Her neighbours are well-known designers such as David Linley and Christopher Hodsoll. Appley says: "Of course there is a great choice of antique furniture from all over the world, but I'm a real Francophile. My love of all things French started a long time ago when I was at the Sorbonne as a student.

"As well as taking great care to buy the right pieces, usually from France, but sometimes from England, Sweden and other countries, it is important for us to make sure all the items complement each other. That's why we take such care displaying everything. We try to make pictures.

"We feel that the shop fits really well in this area, which is famous for its antique shops. It has the sort of village atmosphere that perfectly suits my pieces, from Louis XVI-style chairs and a 19th-century dresser to garden sculptures and, of course, Zoë's flowers.

"It's very exciting running the shop. We get a lot of eccentric customers, they're lovely. You never know who will come into the shop next, but I'm never any good at recognising anyone famous. Zoë tells me who they are after they have left the shop. Luckily, she is always by my side.

"Apart from the day-to-day thrills, one of the highlights of the year is our garden exhibition, which we run at the same time as the Chelsea Flower Show in May. The flowers, the rustic feel, things for the garden, everything comes together.

Shepherds
Creativity between the covers

"It's an odd shop, really, because of all the different things we do. A lot of people say this is their favourite shop. What they mean is they have never seen anything like it. We make things on the premises and there is a feeling of craftsmanship. Most shops in London have lost that element of creativity," says Rob Shepherd.

Like a shop in a Charles Dickens story, every corner of Shepherds Bookbinders on Rochester Row yields a treasure, from hand-bound books and intricate Japanese papers to some exotic ink or a craftsman's tiny tools. Its work, sought after by museums and book enthusiasts around the world, includes book sales and restorations as well as binding courses.

The shop was founded in 1988 by managing director Shepherd,who started work as a self-employed bookbinder in 1976. It joined forces with two famous names of the bookbinding world in 1998: Zaehnsdorf, which started business in 1842; and Sangorski & Sutcliffe, set up in 1901 and well known for its spectacular jewelled bindings. Shepherd says: "I have always been fascinated by bookbinding and its history. Getting together with Zaehnsdorf and Sangorski

& Sutcliffe was particularly exciting, because they have such interesting histories. In 1911 Sangorski & Sutcliffe produced a jewelled binding of the Rubai'yat of Omar Khayyám, known as the *Great Omar*, which went down with the Titanic.

"Some of the books we work on are hundreds of years old, sometimes dating back to the 16th century, and they can often be extremely valuable. A lot of our work is for the royal palaces, major museums and auction houses worldwide and one of the main reasons for siting the shop in Victoria was to be central to the major museums and auction houses in London.

"Not all of our work is for institutions though. Many of our customers are individuals who love books or may have a book that is precious to them – perhaps an old bible – that needs restoring. The cost of restoring a book might be £300 for a 19th-century bible or a lot more expensive for something particularly intricate.

"Restorations can take many, many hours of painstaking work. It takes many years of experience to become a top restorer and our craftsmen are dedicated to creating the best fine binding in the world. That's rare in today's world and that's why people love the shop.

Westminster Abbey

Tradition has it that the Abbey dates from the seventh century, but Edward the Confessor consecrated a new church on the site in 1065. Six kings are buried in the Abbey's shrine of St Edward, including Edward III, whose sombre gilt bronze effigy dates to 1377

The Political Village

Parliament is at the centre of a web of political institutions all within walking distance of each other. Iain Dale explains. Drawings by Andre Carrilho

Touching in its majesty
Parliament's Victorian Gothic river frontage
marks one boundary of a thriving, gossipy
community obsessed with politics. Winston
Churchill (left) remains the all-time master of
the great Parliamentary occasion

The mantle of history
Although political obsessives are preoccupied
by the latest policy debate or scandal,
the shades of centuries of Parliamentary history
are all around them. When he took office
in 1997, Tony Blair (below) was the youngest
prime minister since 1812

Drive from Trafalgar Square up the Mall to Buckingham Palace, then head left down Vauxhall Bridge Road. You come to the River Thames and turn left along the Embankment past the Millbank Tower, past the Houses of Parliament and along Whitehall before heading back into Trafalgar Square. You've just driven round Westminster's political village.

Like any village it's a real community, full of life, full of characters and above all, full of gossip. Because that's what makes the political world buzz – gossip, with a little bit of intrigue thrown in for good measure. And who better to provide it than a wonderful mixture of politicians, lobbyists, political journalists, think-tank policy wonks and the whole gamut of political obsessives. Where else in Britain would you find such people rubbing shoulders in such a confined area? The Westminster political village is special, and its inhabitants rarely let you forget it.

Nothing forms the character of a community better than the buildings which it inhabits. And in the Westminster village the old and the new rub together somewhat uncomfortably. Alongside the Gothic splendour of the Houses of Parliament and the imposing majesty of Westminster Abbey, the modern design of the Queen Elizabeth Conference Centre sits rather uneasily. But opposite Big Ben the £800 million Portcullis House provides sanctuary for busy MPs and their staffs. The design of the building, although modern in style, somehow fits alongside the Dickensian St Stephen's Tavern, recently reopened with the same fittings which were to be found there a century ago.

Many Westminster villagers cheered loudly when the ugly 1960s tower blocks which had housed the Departments of Transport and the Environment were demolished at the turn of the millennium, but many local residents could be forgiven for hoping that this was just the beginning. The characterless buildings which now reside on each side of Victoria Street hardly do justice to one of Westminster's main thoroughfares, but veer off Victoria Street and there are untold treasures to find.

Some of Westminster's most famous residents live in the streets behind Westminster School. Cowley Street, Lord North Street and Gayfere Street play host to the rich and infamous. The Liberal Democrats feel that their Cowley Street HQ address gives them a kudos the Conservatives will find hard to replicate when they move from their ancestral Smith Square home to a modern office in Victoria Street

above a Starbucks. Labour moved recently in the opposite direction, from the imposing Millbank Tower to a Victorian block in Old Queen Street.

So what kind of person inhabits the Westminster village? All forms of human life – from the dosser to the duke – live in the village. Like any village it has its fair share of eccentrics and they make it what it is – a shining example of people from all walks of life co-existing in a relatively small space of land and allowing each other to get on with their lives. But the village is rather like one of those sleepy north Norfolk villages which are empty during the week, just waiting in anticipation for the floods of incomers at the weekend who descend on the area to visit their second homes. Except that in the case of the Westminster village it is the other way around. At the weekend the village is empty. In some areas you can almost hear the tumbleweed rolling down the street. If it weren't for the constant babble of the tourists, no matter what time of year it is, some streets would be totally devoid of human life. But during the week the streets palpably throb with vibrancy from dawn until deep into the night.

Permanent Secretaries rub shoulders with junior officials. Cabinet Ministers walk from their departments to the Commons. Lobbyists scurry along looking for some corridors of power to walk down. Journalists skulk in every corner trying to sniff out a story. There's always something going on. It really is a small village and the chances of meeting a famous figure from the world of politics and government on the street are fairly high, no matter what the time of day.

The lady's not for turning
The political village's traditional drinking hole,
St Stephen's Tavern, takes its name from the
clock tower that houses Big Ben.
Many conservatives still yearn for the days
when Margaret Thatcher (below) dominated
Britain's politics

So where does the villager go to eat and drink? Westminster has often been described as a culinary desert, and to a certain extent that remains true today, but a few superb eateries have opened in recent years. The Cinnamon Club is located in the old Westminster Library in Great Smith Street. It's huge. Many thought it was doomed to fail, yet it goes from strength to strength, serving up a wide range of lighter Indian fare in a uniquely British atmosphere.

Another newcomer on the Westminster block is Bank restaurant and bar, which forms part of the Crown Plaza Hotel on Buckingham Gate. It's very American in design – airy, light and bustling – which is why it attracts a youngish crowd containing a mix of the political glitterati and business people. It's not the place to be seen if you're trying to be discreet. The menu is varied and suits most tastes and the staff are efficient and friendly. For the more traditional tastes – roast beef and jam roly poly – Shepherd's in Marsham Street remains very popular, particularly among MPs and lobbyists. It's part owned by actor Michael Caine. Another favourite haunt is Gran Paradiso in Wilton Road, where the Italian host is sure to beam out a welcoming smile.

Politicians keep very different hours compared to a few years ago. Since the introduction of so-called family-friendly debating hours the House of Commons' club-like atmosphere has diminished as MPs seek their evening's entertainment elsewhere. Some seek solace in food, others in drink.

The area is rich with pubs, some for the tourists but most for locals. The

Speaker in Great Peter Street would seem to be aimed at the former but is actually only frequented by the latter. The Marquess of Granby in Smith Square has a great history of being a place of political intrigue, as it is the local for Conservative Central Office and until recently the Transport & General Workers' Union. The Red Lion on Whitehall is a pub where tourists and politicos mix uneasily. It is renowned as the place where former spin doctor Charlie Whelan famously barked out the Government's European policy to a disbelieving Prime Minister Tony Blair on his mobile phone. The newly refurbished St Stephen's Tavern opposite Big Ben attracts rafts of beleaguered House of Commons secretaries and researchers. It has also become a favourite of the Westminster lobby journalists. You can positively hear the sound of ears flapping

as they try to pick up the latest morsel of gossip from an unsuspecting secretary.

For those seeking out the traditional political clubs, the Westminster village itself is pretty barren. Apart from the splendid National Liberal Club in Whitehall Place, most of the gentlemen's clubs of old are located just over the other side of St James's Park in Pall Mall. But the National Liberal Club itself is a treasure. It is slightly less stuffy than the Reform Club and the Carlton, yet it has retained its air of 19th-century tradition, with the huge bust of Gladstone glowering down at those trying to digest the indifferent fare in the dining room. The Library is something to behold, and an ideal place to grab a mid-afternoon snooze among the magnificent paintings of forgotten Liberal leaders such as Sir Archibald Sinclair and Jo Grimond.

Bizarrely, although the Westminster village is a prime tourist area, there isn't actually a lot for visitors to do apart from wander the streets in wonder. The Cabinet War Rooms located under the Foreign Office are being transformed into a shrine to Winston Churchill – quite right, too – and are particularly popular with Americans. The Palace of Westminster itself is only just waking up to its tremendous potential for the tourist market. There are now guided tours when Parliament is not in session.

So whether you live in the village, work in it or are a visitor, it soon becomes clear that it's a unique place, with a unique history. It doesn't take kindly to change and it cherishes its traditions. You can be at the centre of the nation's life yet at the same time be a million miles away. It's what makes it so special.

From major multinationals to entrepreneurial start-ups, Lance Knobel finds a wide range of businesses in Victoria. Photographs by Red Saunders

Neighbours

Sir Stuart Hampson, chairman, John Lewis Partnership
John Lewis is one of Britain's largest retailers and is still run along the cooperative principles established by John Spedan Lewis

Some city areas are indelibly associated with particular industries. If you are seeking large financial institutions, London's City rivals New York's Wall Street as a global centre. In advertising, New York's Madison Avenue identifies the industry, even if many agencies have moved to other parts of midtown.

Victoria defies such easy identification. Headquarters for large industrial groups are down the street from major retailers who are around the corner from media groups. Smaller companies can be found throughout Victoria as well, from the oldest car garage in London to a speciality cheese supplier. The only industry that can lay claim to large parts of Victoria is government. The historic heart of British government is in Whitehall, but many ministries outgrew that one street long ago. Victoria has proved to be the logical home for many of them, thanks to its proximity to both Parliament and the locus of power in Downing Street.

Perhaps the most resonant corporate name in Victoria is Rolls-Royce. As the company's executives get tired of saying, however, the famous cars are not their business. Instead, Rolls-Royce is one of the world's major aerospace groups. It is the direct descendant of the meeting in 1904 of railway apprentice Henry Royce and car dealer Charles Rolls. The cars, manufactured by BMW since 1998, have to license the brand name from the aerospace group.

From the headquarters just off Victoria Street, Rolls-Royce executives have forged one of the major manufacturing success stories of recent decades in Britain. Over the past 20 years, the company has quadrupled its share of the global aviation business. It is the world's second largest maker of engines for commercial aircraft after GE, and number one for power systems for defence aircraft and marine propulsion. Former chairman Sir Ralph Robins proudly notes, "There are very few British companies that are 100 years old and are still able to say they are a world player."

Peter Gibbon, managing director, MGA Advertising
From its origins as a business-to-business agency, MGA now handles a full range of clients, with particular strengths in government work

**Mike Salamon,
group president,
non-ferrous metals,
BHP Billiton**
The world's largest
resources company,
BHP Billiton maintains
two headquarters, in
London's Victoria and
Australia's Victoria –
Melbourne

**Andrew Walmsley
and Charles Dobres,
COO and CEO, i-Level**
Specialisation has
made i-Level the
largest digital media
agency in the UK

Another Victoria corporate resident dates its origins to the midst of the era of Queen Victoria. John Lewis Partnership is one of the UK's largest retailers, with 26 department stores and 141 supermarkets. But it is its unique corporate structure that sets it apart from its rivals. The group is Britain's largest employee cooperative, with over 59,000 staff – the Partners.

The group dates back to a small draper's shop opened in Oxford Street in 1864. It grew into a large department store by 1905 and such was its success that it was able to acquire a failing rival, Peter Jones in Chelsea, to double the company's size. The original Mr Lewis gave his son, John Spedan Lewis, control of Peter Jones in 1914. It was the young Mr Lewis who conceived the idea of a cooperative, which he finally created in 1929. His business philosophy was baldly stated: "The supreme purpose of the John Lewis Partnership is simply the happiness of its members." His vision has proved remarkably successful.

Years of steady, consistent growth have led to a group with a turnover of £4.7 billion and profits of £108 million. In the most recent year, £67 million of that profit was paid as a bonus to the Partners. The cooperative ethos suffuses everything about John Lewis. Visitors to its headquarters can pick up a copy of the in-house magazine, *Gazette*, and without fail find chairman Sir Stuart Hampson responding personally to letters from other Partners.

Around the corner from John Lewis Partnership's headquarters is the London base of BHP Billiton, the world's largest resources company. It resulted from the 2001 merger of Australian giant BHP and London-based Billiton. The group maintains a dual listing in Australia and London, although its structure is completely integrated.

In addition to the corporate functions necessary to tend the London listing, two of the group's divisions – energy and non-ferrous metals, both multibillion dollar

Vernon Galiffe, manager, Eaton Square Garage
Originally catering for horses and carriages, the garage has retained its traditions of personal service

businesses – are led from the London headquarters overlooking Victoria Station. BHP Billiton's turnover exceeds $17 billion, and its mining and energy operations are in 20 countries around the world.

Victoria's largest groups are often just around the corner from far smaller businesses. Rippon Cheese Stores, founded in 1981, sells over 500 different cheeses from its shop on Upper Tachbrook Street. Founder Philip Rippon left London's oldest cheesemongers, Paxton & Whitfield, to set up his own business with his wife Karen, who left a career in finance to run the business side.

More than 150 years before Rippon Cheese Stores was created, the Eaton Square Garage was already a thriving place to stable horses and horse carriages. Fortunately, at the end of the 19th century the owners spotted the opportunity provided by the new technology of automobiles and the business is still thriving.

More contemporary young and entrepreneurial companies can also be found in Victoria. Red Commerce was founded in 2000 by three 24-year-old friends. The company provides recruitment services for companies seeking expertise in SAP and other enterprise computing. Over the four years since founding, Red Commerce has averaged 130 per cent year-on-year growth. In 2004 it expects turnover to top £15 million, and staff numbers to grow to more than 50.

Ezra Chapman, Red Commerce's 28-year-old CEO, believes the company can continue to defy gravity for a few years yet. "We can continue to grow at our rate for the next two years or so," he says. "We're already recruiting for the next year ahead."

Chapman says that logistically, the company could be located anywhere. "If it had been right to put the company in Scotland, we could have," he says. But London has proved to be ideal in terms of the sales culture and the ready availability of other European speakers. Only 20 per cent

Fru Hazlitt, managing director, Yahoo UK and Ireland
Ten years after its founding by students at Stanford University, Yahoo is one of the world's 100 most valuable brands

of the company's work is for clients in the UK. And Chapman is equally clear why Red Commerce chose Victoria: "Pick up any tube map and it's convenient to everywhere. It gives us the largest catchment area to source the best marketing and sales people."

Although few people associate Victoria with media, there is a nascent media village in the area. From Channel 4 to Random House to Yahoo Europe, significant media companies have chosen Victoria as a base.

One of the youngest major companies in Victoria is also probably one of the best known. Silicon Valley's Yahoo has had its European and UK headquarters in Victoria since 2000. Although barely ten years have passed since Jerry Yang and David Filo started Yahoo in a trailer at Stanford University, it is one of the world's top 100 brands according to *Business Week*. The European base in Victoria houses several hundred staff.

Fru Hazlitt, managing director of Yahoo UK and Ireland, says the company chose Victoria "to be in the centre of it all. We're between the City on one side and all the media agencies in Soho on the other."

On the other side of Victoria, a dramatic building by Richard Rogers & Partners marks the headquarters of Channel 4, the UK's only publicly owned commercial broadcaster. Channel 4 was founded in 1982 with a specific remit to "demonstrate innovation, experimentation and creativity". That remit has been interpreted in a variety of ways: Channel 4 brought *Big Brother* to the UK, and is the UK home of more sophisticated US series like *The Sopranos*, *The West Wing* and *Sex and the City*.

What is particularly innovative in the UK context is that, unlike the BBC or the major ITV companies, Channel 4 does not produce its own programmes. Instead it commissions them from over 300 independent production companies. The rise of Channel 4 has been a major factor in the growth of creative, independent producers in the UK.

Ezra Chapman, CEO, Red Commerce
A fast-growing IT recruitment firm, 80 per cent of Red Commerce's revenues come from outside Britain

Media services can also be found in the area. MGA Advertising has particular strengths in business-to-business and government advertising, with clients including aerospace group BAE Systems and the Department of Trade and Industry.

Recent start-up i-Level is already Europe's largest buyer of digital media, and has pioneered the use of mobile telephones for marketing. CEO Charles Dobres says i-Level started in 1999 as an internet media agency, but now, "if it's digital, we do it". The company has grown each year and currently has 53 staff. It is now expanding into other European markets. Dobres says 10 per cent of i-Level's business is outside the UK and growing fast.

It isn't just new media stars that have clustered in Victoria. Random House has its UK headquarters around the corner from the Tate Gallery. The world's largest English-language trade book publisher, Random House was founded in New York in 1925 by Bennett Cerf and Donald Klopfer when they purchased The Modern Library, a publisher of reprint classics. Perhaps its proudest literary moment came when it defended the US publication of James Joyce's masterpiece *Ulysses*. In Britain, Random House is the result of the acquisition of a number of famous publishers, including Chatto & Windus, Bodley Head, Jonathan Cape and Century Hutchinson in the 1980s. Random House is now a subsidiary of German media giant Bertelsmann.

Gail Rebuck, chairman and CEO of Random House UK, is a particularly eloquent defender of the traditional book against its new media rivals. In a recent speech, she noted, "despite the very real pressures and the new technologies, I do not believe the apocalyptic predictions will be realised. I am optimistic about the book industry and the future of books because, in their unflamboyant way, books penetrate the cynicism, confusion and anxiety of the age."

Philip and Karen Rippon, Rippon Cheese Stores
The Rippons stock over 500 cheeses in their shop on Upper Tachbrook Street

The Royal Horticultural Society

The RHS has been encouraging gardeners for over
200 years. The Lindley Library in its Vincent Square
headquarters houses more than 50,000 books and
18,000 horticultural drawings, such as this 18th-century
'Vandewill' iris by W Curtis

Belgravia's grand terraces and garden squares still reflect the extraordinary vision of Thomas Cubitt, writes Alan Powers. Photographs by Phil Sayer

Perfect Square

When King George III bought Buckingham House in 1762, a slow-burning fuse was lit which, some 60 years later, detonated the construction of Belgravia. Buckingham House became Buckingham Palace, and in 1821, when the post-Waterloo boom economy in Britain was at full strength, Earl Grosvenor having first commissioned a plan from the architect James Wyatt in 1812, decided it was finally time to develop the Five Fields. It was a place of poorly drained clay soil, known for its asparagus, forming one of several pockets of open land strangely close to the centres of wealth and power in London. The pattern of development at the time tended to consist of sudden leap-frog moves into distant fields, followed by a more systematic backfilling of the spaces between.

The Grosvenor family already knew something about urban development. In 1677 the Cheshire Baronet, Sir Thomas Grosvenor, married the 12-year-old Mary Davies, heiress not only to 100 acres in Mayfair, but a further 300 acres of what is now Belgravia and Pimlico. The latter was an old place-name covering the whole district, whereas Belgravia is a made-up name, derived from Belgrave Square, named in turn after the village of Belgrave in Cheshire, another part of Grosvenor's Estate.

The development of the Mayfair estate was complete when Sir Thomas's successor, Robert Grosvenor, the first Marquess of Westminster, began to see the potential of his other property. Already in the 1770s the area bordering Sloane Street, on Lord Cadogan's land, had been developed as Hans Town, with the old village of Chelsea beyond it. The King's Road, leading from St James's to Hampton Court and Kew and before 1830 still a private road, gave a clue to the geometry of a future street pattern, including the diagonal alignment of Belgrave Square which featured in Wyatt's plan. Eaton Square, named after the Grosvenor seat in Cheshire, was the brainchild of the architect-surveyors

Alexander and Daniel Robertson in 1813, an urban "parkway" flanking the King's Road and unparalleled elsewhere in London for its breadth and leafiness. Its southern side is effectively the southern boundary of Belgravia proper.

The practice of development in London was for the ground landlord to let sites, normally for 99 years, to individual investors or syndicates. Because of the capital-intensive works needed at the start of any major urban project, including constructing sewers, making up roads and providing street lighting, house building was a long-term investment compared to the safe returns on government stock. It was all too common for builders to finish a house with the appearance of quality, only for defects to emerge over time. Estate managers and surveyors also needed to act for the long-term interests of the ground landlord. The physical matrix of the streets and squares, with their mews properties to the rear, could not easily be

Upstairs downstairs
The imposing black doors in Belgravia still suggest the residences of the grand families of the Victorian era. All buildings are required by the Grosvenor Estate to maintain the cream colour of the terraces (overleaf)

Garden in the city
Eaton Square (above, right and overleaf) remains unparalleled in London for its breadth and leafiness. It was conceived in 1813 as an urban parkway flanking the King's Road

changed later on, and even small changes of use had to be strictly controlled to maintain the tone of the area.

Belgravia is especially associated with the builder and developer Thomas Cubitt (1788-1855), who in 1824 took a large area of land, sharing the spoils with another builder, Seth Smith. Before Belgravia, Cubitt had developed the Bedford Estate in Bloomsbury, the district whose claim to high fashion Belgravia soon stole away. Early in his career, Cubitt decided to employ directly all the principal tradesmen rather than sub-contracting, as had been the time-honoured practice. His establishment in Gray's Inn Road represented the highest standard of materials and work anywhere in Britain at the time. He also had an eye for design, and his younger brother Lewis practised as an architect. He understood the need to create top-quality infrastructure for Belgravia from the beginning, even though it was not the easiest land to build on and to drain.

The architectural attribution of Belgravia is historically complex. Cubitt and Seth Smith passed on the responsibility for Belgrave Square itself to another syndicate led by the Swiss Haldimand brothers. They employed the architect George Basevi, a pupil of Sir John Soane, to design the main elevations. Cubitt's biographer, Hermione Hobhouse, sees this move in terms of his understanding that the overall quality of the area mattered most, viewing the deal as "quite compatible with a man who cared for the architectural standing of the whole area but without personal ambition". The grand square could take care of itself, but Cubitt would better be able to keep up the quality in the surrounding streets.

Basevi, whose chief work is the Fitzwilliam Museum in Cambridge, was an architect of the Regency period with a scholarly approach to borrowing classical details from ancient Greece. The choice of stucco (hard exterior plaster) as a finish for the brick-built terraces

was probably a foregone conclusion following John Nash's successful introduction of this material in Regent's Park.

The buildings would not, however, have originally been finished in the cream-coloured oil paint of today, but in imitation of the yellow ochre of Bath Stone, the material out of which Nash constructed his portions of Buckingham Palace. Either way, stucco held the field in London building until the revival of red brick in the 1880s, and Londoners are grateful for the luminosity it provides in all the varied conditions of light throughout the year. The unified colour is still strictly specified by Grosvenor for all householders.

The ten acres of Belgrave Square, including 4.5 acres of garden, offer an apt balance of openness and enclosure, with the unusual treatment of three of the corners as sites for large individual villas. On the north side of Eaton Square, we can see the gradual transformation of Regency architectural

Grecian forms
The consistent repetition of classical forms creates the grandeur and beauty of Belgravia. The continuous colonnades of the ground floor (right) create a balcony above, from which delectable greenery occasionally bursts out

taste, which emphasises the unity of a terrace of houses in the composition of one single 'palace' frontage, into early Victorian. Pilasters and columns are abandoned and the Italianate manner, introduced into London by the architect Charles Barry at the Reform Club in Pall Mall, accounts for the familiar conjunction of a deep bracketed cornice with more emphatic quoins emphasising the projecting corners. Still, both the westerly ranges are distinguished by their continuous colonnades attached to the ground floor. These create a running balcony above, parts of which are bowered in delectable-looking greenery.

With these minor variations in style, the lesson of Belgravia remains one of essential consistency with scope for variety. Modern architecture has left relatively little mark. Changes in land ownership are usually apparent where the direction of the streets alters to align with the grid of the Cadogan and Lowndes estates, the latter also largely

developed by Thomas Cubitt. The Ebury Street area pre-dates Belgravia, providing a broad buffer of smaller buildings against the commercial world of Buckingham Palace Road.

Whatever happens behind the black-painted front doors, each exterior still speaks of a single dwelling unit, and as in Georgian London, each size of house has a visual and proportional relationship to all those above or below it in the hierarchy. This carries down to the level of the mews, although these have their own attractive urban scale of narrow width relative to their length, and a generous amount of open sky in the funnel shape between the backs of the full-height terraces. The mews were built as service accommodation for horses and carriage, and intended to be hidden. Cubitt gave them each a fine arched entrance to match the doubtless impeccable turn out of the private carriages which would be seen arriving and departing for duty. When the horse was replaced by the

horseless carriage, the mews might be found harbouring motor cars.

After the Second World War, mews houses became the height of fashion, with brightly painted front doors and tubs of evergreen plants standing on the granite setts of the pavement-less roadway. It is in the mews that you find the majority of pubs of Belgravia, but they are worth finding. The Star in Belgrave Mews West and The Grenadier in Wilton Row both date from 1830, and were discreetly positioned for the servants of the grand houses, and remain unshowy today.

The big estates were wary of allowing shops to invade their precincts. While a few charming period shop-fronts remain in Motcomb Street, the chief commercial activity took place away from view in the Halkin Arcade, the predecessor of a luxury shopping mall, and now filled by Waitrose. The shop windows in its neighbourhood testify to the residents' need for those staple commodities: art, hairdressing and patisserie.

The Royal Court Theatre

Mary Ure and Alan Bates in the landmark 1956
production of John Osborne's 'Look Back in Anger'.
The Royal Court Theatre on Sloane Square continues
to be Britain's leading national company dedicated
to new work by innovative writers

Lunch
in the Park

When the sun comes out, St James's Park
is a popular haven for Victoria's office workers.
Photographs by Elisabeth Scheder-Bieschin

Ducks and dalliances
At lunchtime, visitors to the park might indulge in a
picnic, feed the ducks, admire the flowers, take a gentle walk
or even have a midday nap on the grass

Spies' rendezvous
The park's lake is home to many wild breeds of ducks and birds, including black swans and pelicans. St James's Park is also a common meeting place for fictional spies and their contacts, including John Le Carre's George Smiley and Richard Hannay from 'The 39 Steps'

Table for two
Inn the Park, the recently opened restaurant, offers a
curved wooden terrace overlooking the lake. More traditionally,
deck chairs (right) are available for resting or listening
to band concerts

Royal connections

St James's is the oldest royal park in London, having been created as Henry VIII's deer park in 1532. Three palaces surround the park: Buckingham, St James's and Westminster

Tate Britain is one of the world's greatest art galleries, but sometimes it is the combination of audience and art that is interesting, as photographer Nick Turpin discovers

Private View

GUARD

NO HANDS

LEGS

YOUNG TURNER

LUCKY

HATS

AUDREY

TITANS

TREES

Victoria in Detail

Where to find the shops,
restaurants and institutions
featured in the book

St James's Park

Buckingham
Palace

Grosvenor Crescent

7

Belgrave

Square

8

Westminster Bridge

12

Old Palace Yard

14

Buckingham Gate

Buckingham Gate

22

1

Grosvenor Place

Grosvenor Place

Great Smith Street

16

Victoria Street

9

Hobart Place

Grosvenor Gardens

25

Bressenden Place

18

Victoria Street

Marsham Street

24

Pont Street

Belgrave Place

BELGRAVIA

4

Millbank

Lambeth Brid

Eaton Square

Eccleston Street

Victoria
Station

Wilton Road

13

Horseferry Road

WESTMINSTER

2

Eccleston Bridge

23

Rochester Row

15

Westminster
School
Playing
Field

20

21

10

VICTORIA

11

Vauxhall Bridge Road

19

Sloane
Square

Lower Sloane Street

3

Buckingham Palace Road

Belgrave Road

John Islip Street

Millbank

5

6

17

Pimlico Road

Warwick Way

Ebury Bridge

Chelsea Bridge Road

Ebury Bridge Road

Bessborough Street

Vauxhall Bridge

Lupus Street

Lupus Street

PIMLICO

Grosvenor Road

Grosvenor Road

Chelsea Bridge

RIVER THAMES

0   500m   1000m (1km)

Culture and entertainment

1

Blewcoat School, National Trust Gift Shop and Information Centre
23 Caxton Street
London
SW1H 0PY
020 7222 2877
www.nationaltrust.org.uk/region/thameschilterns

2

Boisdale
13-15 Eccleston Street
London SW1W 9LX
020 7730 6922
www.boisdale.co.uk

3

Royal Court Theatre
Sloane Square
London
SW1W 8AS
Box office 020 7565 5000
www.royalcourttheatre.com

4

St John's, Smith Square
Smith Square
London
SW1P 3HA
020 7222 2168
Box office 020 7222 1061
www.sjss.org.uk

5

Tate Britain
Millbank
London
SW1P 4RG
Switchboard 020 7887 8000
Ticket office and membership
services 020 7887 8888
Recorded information
020 7887 8008
www.tate.org.uk

Eating and drinking

6

Farmers' Market
Orange Square, corner of
Pimlico Road and Ebury Street
Saturday 9am-1pm
www.lfm.org.uk/pimlico

7

The Grenadier
18 Wilton Row
London SW1X 7NR
020 7235 3074

8

Inn the Park
St James's Park
London
SW1A 2BJ
020 7451 9999
www.innthepark.co.uk

9

Noura
16 Hobart Place
London
SW1W 0HH
020 7235 9444
www.noura-brasseries.co.uk

10

Poilâne
46 Elizabeth Street
London
SW1W 9PA
020 7808 4910
www.poilane.fr

11

Rippon Cheese Stores
26 Upper Tachbrook Street
London SW1V 1SW
020 7931 0628

Places of interest

12

Central Hall Westminster
Storey's Gate
London
SW1H 9NH
020 7222 8010
www.c-h-w.com

13

Channel 4 Television
124 Horseferry Road
London SW1P 2TX
020 7396 4444
www.channel4.com

14

Houses of Parliament
House of Commons
London
SW1A 0AA
House of Lords
London
SW1A 0PW
020 7219 3000
www.parliament.uk

15

Lindley Library
Royal Horticultural Society
80 Vincent Square
London
SW1P 2PE
020 7821 3050
www.rhs.org.uk

16

Westminster Abbey
General information:
The Chapter Office
20 Dean's Yard
Westminster Abbey
London
SW1P 3PA
020 7222 5152
Information desk and
tours: 020 7654 4900
www.westminster-abbey.org

Shopping and services

17

Appley Hoare
30 Pimlico Road
London
SW1W 8LJ
020 7730 7070
www.appleyhoare.com

18

Army & Navy
101 Victoria Street
London
SW1E 6QX
020 7834 1234
www.houseoffraser.co.uk

19

David Mellor
4 Sloane Square
London
SW1W 8EE
020 7730 4259
www.davidmellordesign.com

20

Eaton Square Garage
1 Eaton Mews West
London
SW1W 9ET
020 7235 9900/4521
www.eatonsq-garage.co.uk

21

Philip Treacy
69 Elizabeth Street
London
SW1W 9PJ
020 7730 3992
www.philiptreacy.co.uk

22

Run and Become
42 Palmer Street
London
SW1H 0PH
020 7222 1314
www.runandbecome.com

23

Shepherds
76 Rochester Row
London
SW1P 1JU
020 7620 0060
www.bookbinding.co.uk

24

J Wippell and Company
11 Tufton Street
London
SW1P 3QB
020 7222 4528
www.wippell.com

25

The Goring
Beeston Place
London
SW1W 0JW
020 7396 9000
www.goringhotel.co.uk

Published by
Duck Publishing
Studio 6
The Lux Building
2-4 Hoxton Square
London
N1 6NU

© Duck Publishing 2004
ISBN 0-9548191-0-1

Designed by
Esterson Associates

Production management by
Martin Lee

Printed by
Mondadori Printing, Verona, Italy

Edited by
Lance Knobel

With contributions from
Daniel Lee
Iain Dale
Alan Powers

Research by
Hannah Tyson
Kamalakshi Mehta

Photography and illustration by
Phil Sayer
Simon Wheeler
Lucinda Rogers
Helen Mellor
Red Saunders
Andre Carrilho
Elisabeth Scheder-Bieschin
Nick Turpin

Picture research by
Suzanne Hodgart

Picture credits
Army & Navy catalogue:
Mary Evans Picture Library
Channel 4: Richard Bryant/Arcaid
Westminster Abbey: Copyright Dean
and Chapter of Westminster
Royal Horticultural Society:
Royal Horticultural Society,
Lindley Library
Royal Court: Copyright
Hulton-Deutsch Collection/Corbis
Aerial photography:
Getmapping plc